START TO FINISH CHICAGO!

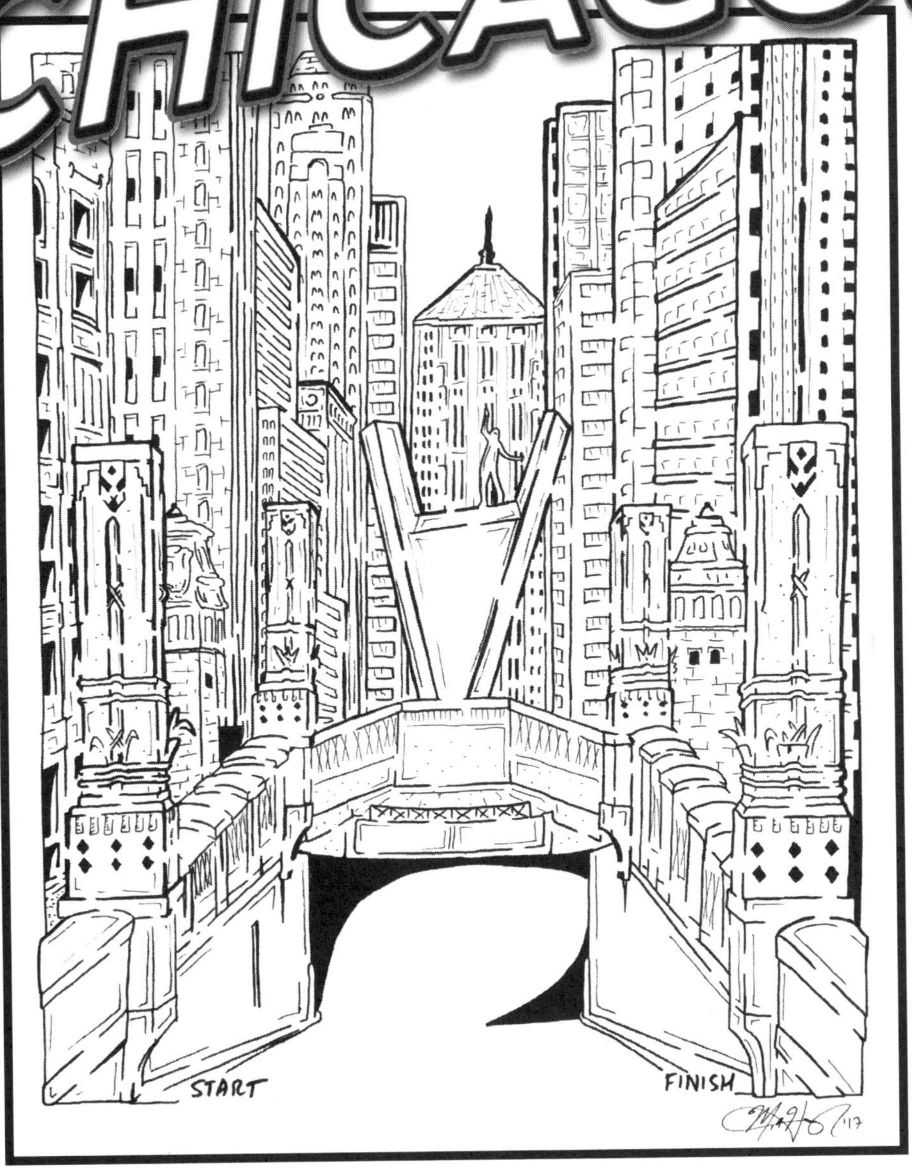

Matthew Haussler

Copyright © 2017 by Reedy Press, LLC
Reedy Press
PO Box 5131
St. Louis, MO 63139, USA
www.reedypress.com

No part of this publication may be reproduced or transmitted in any form or by any means, electronic or mechanical, including photocopy, recording, or any information storage and retrieval system, without permission in writing from the publisher.

Permissions may be sought directly from Reedy Press at the above mailing address or via our website at www.reedypress.com.

ISBN: 9781681060927

Printed in the United States of America
17 18 19 20 21   5 4 3 2 1

1. Addison Red Line CTA
2. Aragon Theater
3. Art Institute Lion
4. Art Institute Path
5. Baha'i Temple
6. Benito Juarez Statue
7. Bloomingdales Medinah Building
8. Britannica Building
9. Calder's Flamingo
10. Chicago Theater
11. Chinatown Gate
12. Chinatown Library
13. Cloud Gate
14. Crain Communications Building
15. Crossing Sculpture
16. Cultural Center Interior
17. Field Museum
18. General John A. Logan Sculpture
19. Grainne Sculpture and Presidential Towers
20. Grant Statue
21. Green Mill
22. Jay Pritzker Pavilion
23. John Hancock Building
24. LaSalle Bridge
25. Lincoln Park Conservatory
26. Lincoln Park Zoo Zebra
27. Lyric Opera Building
28. Macy's Clock
29. Macy's Fountain
30. Marina City
31. Mary Bartelme Park
32. Merchandise Mart
33. Navy Pier Ferris Wheel
34. Old Saint Patrick
35. Picasso Sculpture
36. Planetarium
37. San Marco II
38. Tiffany Dome
39. United Station
40. Watertower
41. White Sox
42. Willis Tower from the South
43. Willis Tower
44. Wrigley Building
45. Wrigley Field

Mazes have existed in various forms over the centuries. They have captivated minds and aided in pensive reflection. Over the past few years, I've taken this ancient puzzle and twisted it into something exciting and new.

Welcome to a fun and engaging way to see the world! Each of the forty five mazes in *Start to Finish Chicago!* is a hand-drawn, solvable puzzle for you to enjoy. This large compilation of brand new pieces will entertain and intrigue you for hours.

—Matthew Haussler

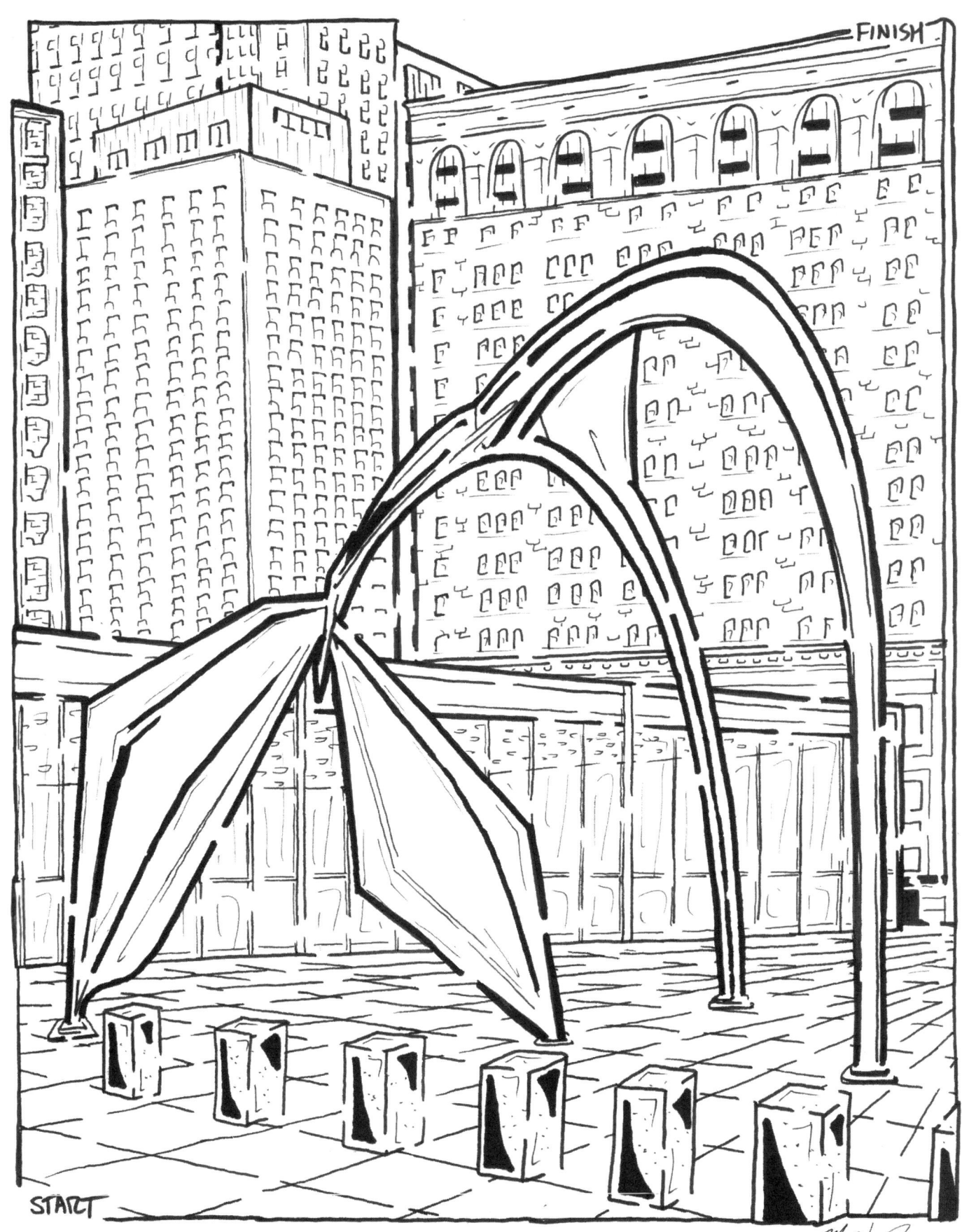

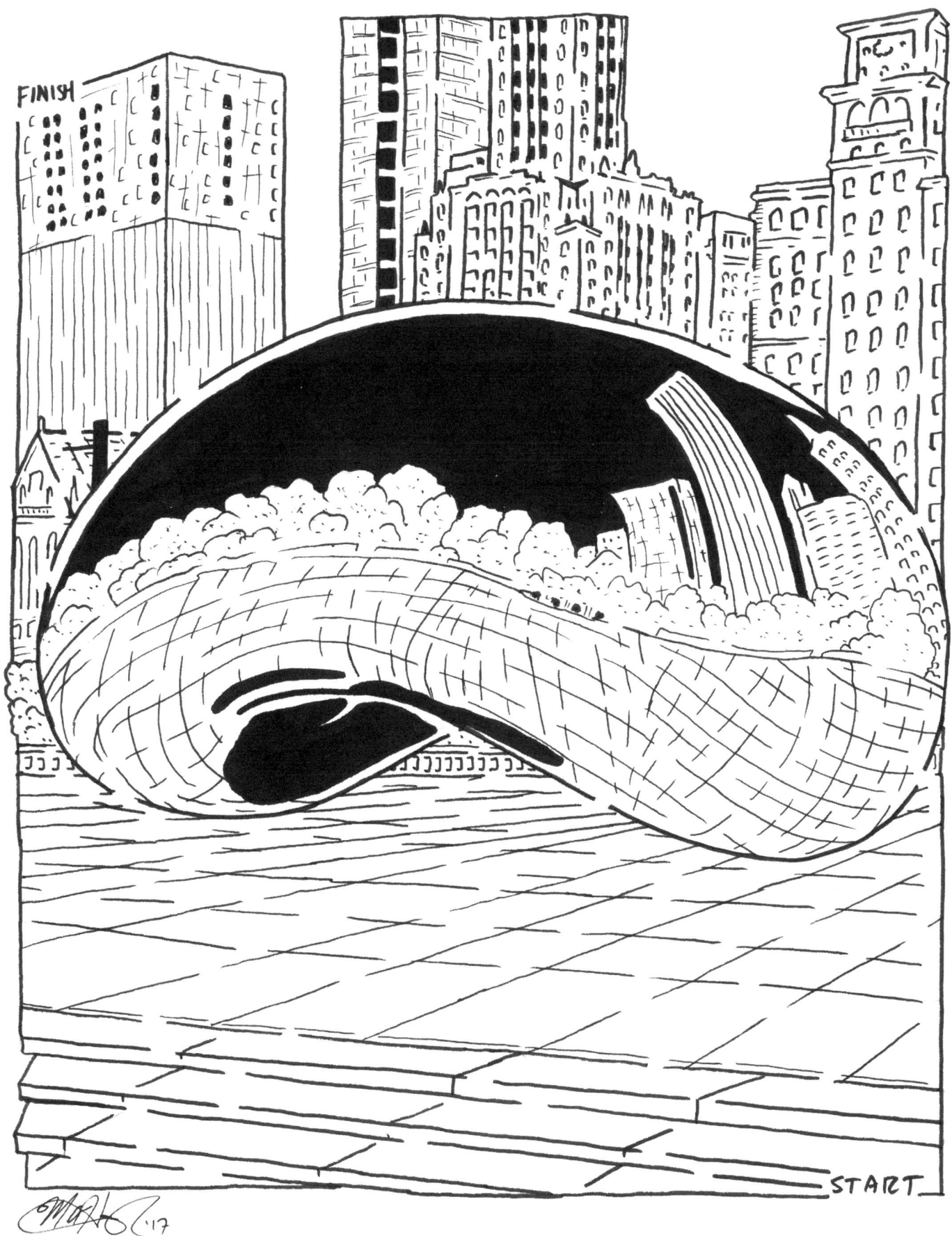

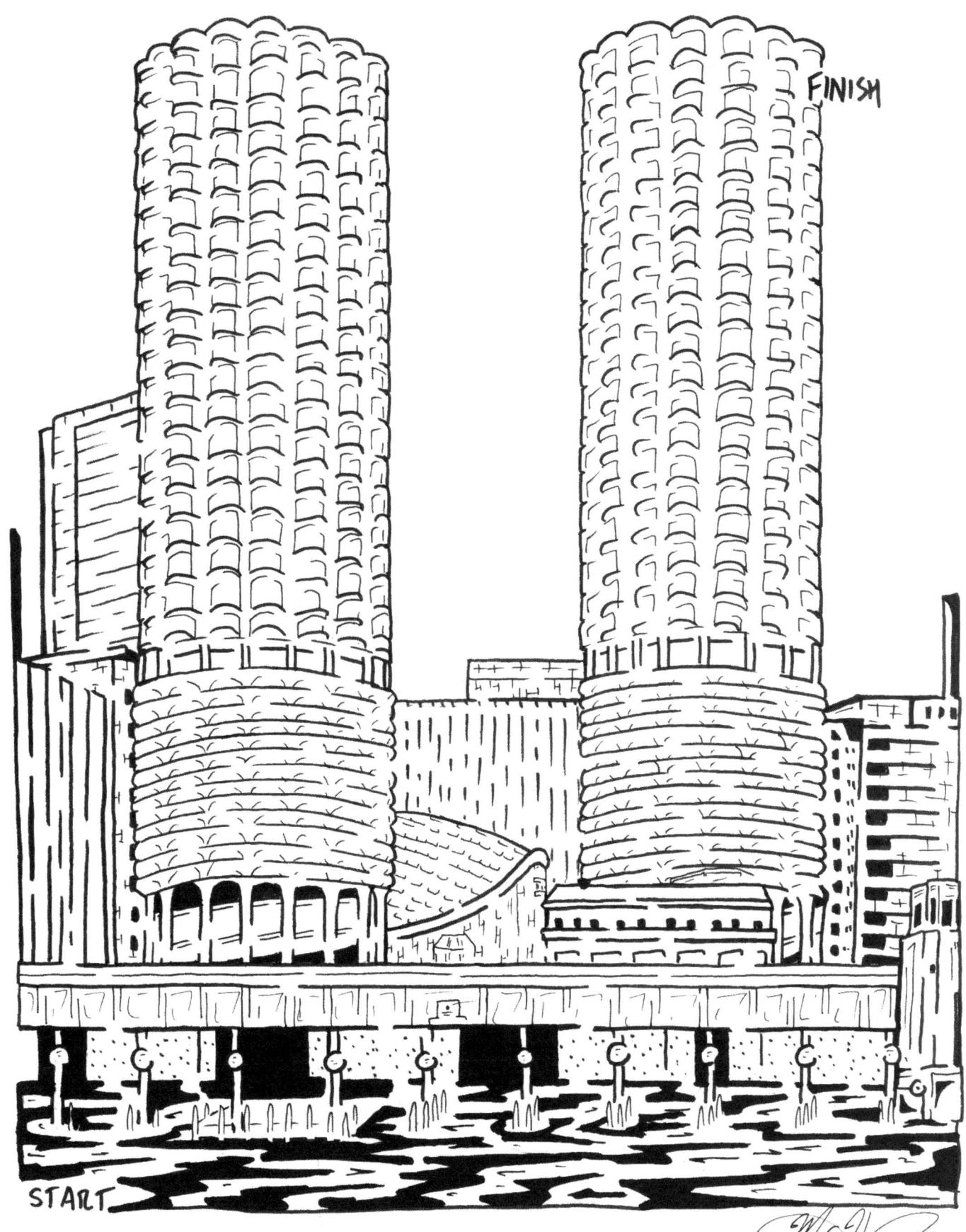

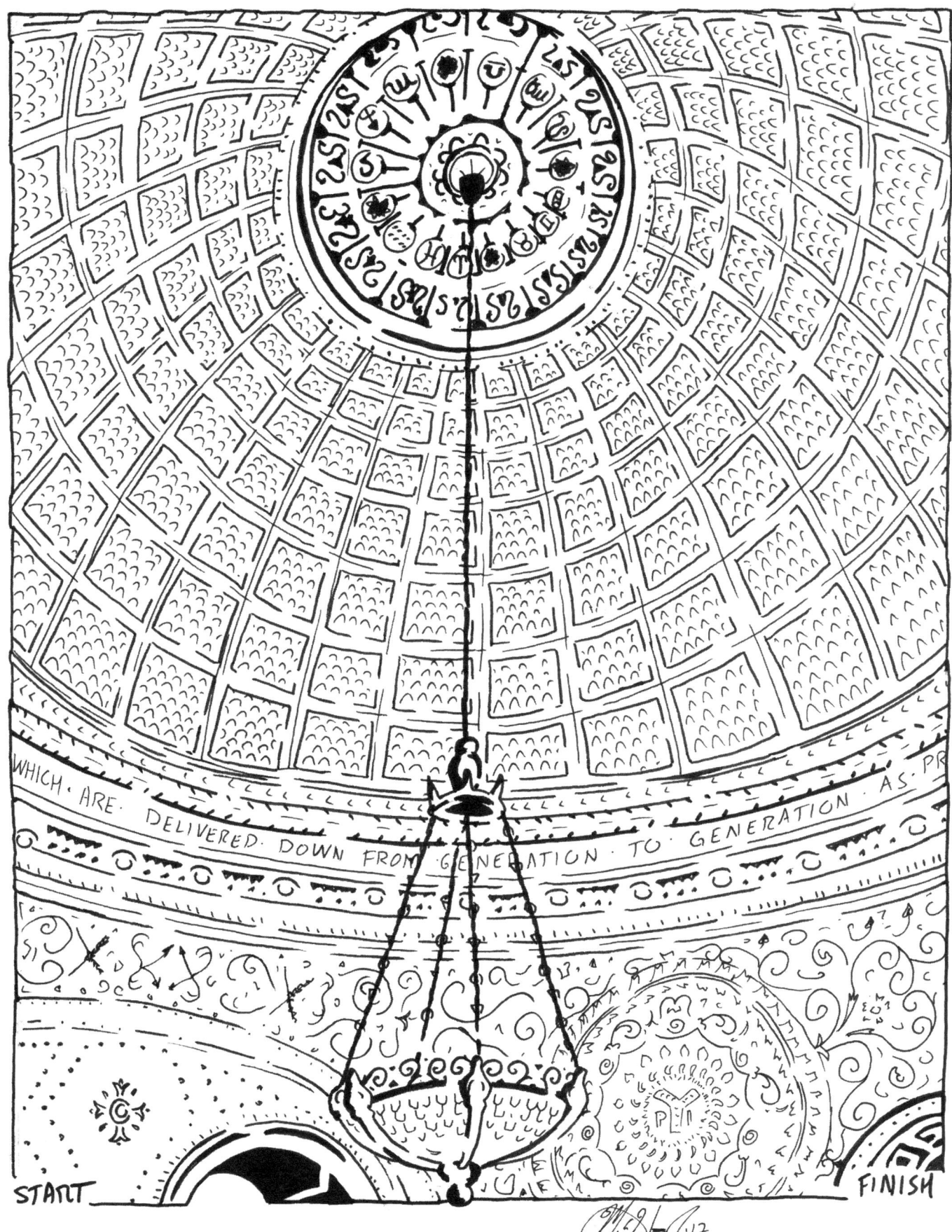

Maze Solutions

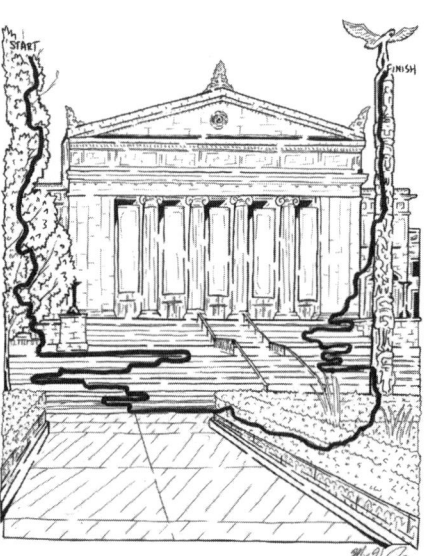

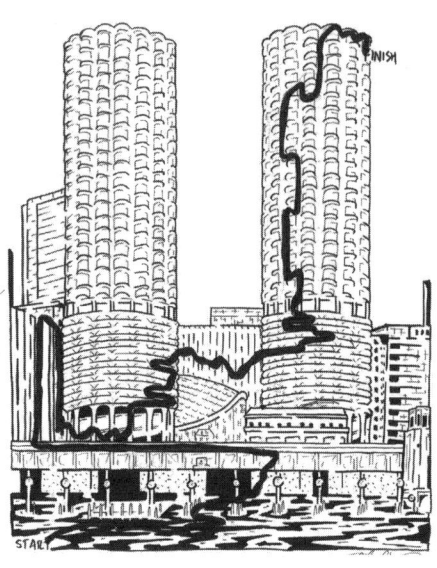

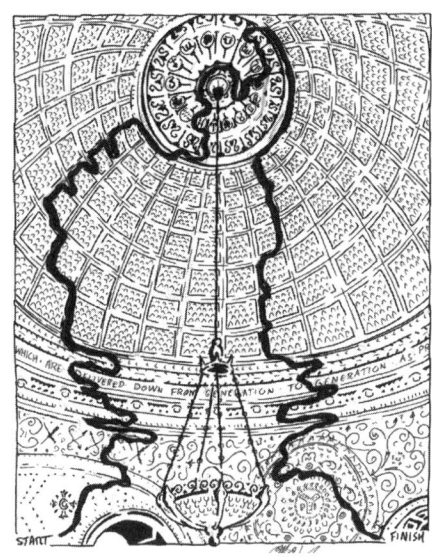